BOY SCOUTS OF AMERICA
MERIT BADGE SERIES

COLLECTIONS

"Enhancing our youths' competitive edge through merit badges"

BOY SCOUTS OF AMERICA®

Requirements

1. Prepare a short written report or outline for your counselor, giving a detailed description of your collection,* including a short history. Be sure to include why you chose that particular type of collecting and what you enjoy and have learned from your collection.*
2. Explain the growth and development of your collection.
3. Demonstrate your knowledge of preserving and displaying your collection.
    a. Explain the precautions you need to take to preserve your collection, including
        (1) Handling
        (2) Cleaning
        (3) Storage
    b. Explain how best to display your collection, keeping in mind preserving as discussed above.
    c. Explain to your counselor the events available for a hobbyist of this collection, including shows, seminars, conventions, contests, and museum programs and exhibits.
4. Demonstrate your knowledge of collecting and investing. Discuss with your counselor:
    a. How investing and speculation would apply to your collection
    b. What you would look for in purchasing other collections similar to yours
    c. What you would expect in return value if you decided to sell all or part of the collection

*Stamp and coin collecting are excluded from eligibility for this merit badge.

35875
ISBN 978-0-8395-3242-2
©2013 Boy Scouts of America
2022 Printing

5. Do the following:

    a. Discuss with your counselor at least 10 terms commonly used in your collection and be prepared to discuss the definition of each.

    b. Show your counselor any two groups from your collection. Explain how you organized your collection and why you chose that method. (Note: If your collection is too large to transport and your counselor is unable to view your collection directly, photographs should be available to share.)

    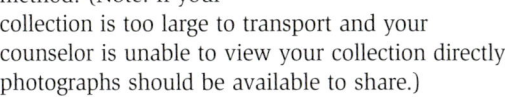

    c. Explain how your collection is valued by other collectors, and display to your counselor any price guides that may be available.

    d. Explain how your collection is graded for value, physical defects, size, and age. Show the various classifications or ratings used in your collection.

    e. List the national, state, or local association responsive to your collection.

    f. Show the location of and explain to your counselor the identification number (if applicable), series, brand name (if any), and any other special identification marks.

6. Discuss with your counselor the plans you have to continue with the collection in the future.

7. Discuss with your counselor why and how collecting has changed and how this applies to your collection.

8. Find out about career opportunities in collecting. Pick one and find out the education, training, and experience required for this profession. Discuss this with your counselor, and explain why this profession might interest you.

Contents

Treasure Hunts and Paper Chases. 7

Collecting Odds and Ends 19

Comic Books: Collecting Superheroes and Villains 25

Sports Cards: Collecting Athletes 39

Rocks: Collecting Chunks of the Past 51

Careers: From Hobby to Profession 59

Resources for Collecting. 62

Treasure Hunts and Paper Chases

Collecting was once a pastime of the wealthy. Many well-to-do people collected fine art, musical instruments, ancient coins, and rare books. But with the Industrial Revolution in the early 1800s came mass production. Suddenly the new consumer society could afford to buy all kinds of goods.

A collection is not just an accumulation of things, but a well-ordered grouping of several items to be considered as a whole. The collection is worth more than the individual parts.

Don't Lose Your Marbles

Marbles have been found in strange places, including ancient Egyptian tombs. However, most collectible marbles have been produced within the last 160 years. Marbles are made of many substances, including glass, stone, minerals, clay, pottery, porcelain, and china. Some of the first porcelain and china ones were made in the 1840s. Glass marbles became popular in the late 1800s and early 1900s, and mass production of marbles began around the same time. Some rare marbles, which can fetch close to $1,000 each, have names as colorful as they look: popeyes, sparklers, agates, and rainbows.

COLLECTIONS   7

TREASURE HUNTS AND PAPER CHASES

If you enjoy nature, you might collect rocks, fossils, shells, or leaves. If you enjoy sports, you might collect sports cards, baseballs, caps, uniforms, pennants, hockey pucks, or bumper stickers. If toys interest you, so might superhero or action figures, cars, or model airplanes or trains. If military history piques your curiosity, you might collect uniforms, helmets, insignia, medals, flags, or maps.

This pamphlet will give you specific ideas and tips for collecting. You will also find expanded information about comic books, sports cards, and rocks—some of the most popular collectibles.

> In the past, butterfly collecting was a very popular hobby. Collectors captured butterflies and pinned them to boards. Today, however, people prefer to observe butterflies in the same way others "watch" birds—by taking photos and making sketches.

Teachers, librarians, and counselors familiar with your field of collecting can help you find sources to research your ideas.

The die-cast model car craze began in the late 1950s and early 1960s with the introduction of Matchbox cars. The hobby of collecting cars skyrocketed in 1968 when toymaker Mattel launched Hot Wheels. These die-cast metal cars came with special torsion-bar suspension and low-friction wheel bearings, making them the "fastest in the world." Other die-cast brands include Corgi, Dinky, Ertl, Johnny Lightning, Lledo, Racing Champions, Team Caliber, and Tootsie Toy.

8   COLLECTIONS

= Treasure Hunts and Paper Chases

Moving action figures are popular collectibles. Introduced in 1964, G.I. Joe was the first movable action toy in the United States. The World War II soldier came complete with movable limbs and realistic cloth uniforms. In 1970, G.I. Joe figures got realistic hair. Other action figures were introduced during the 1970s, including toys based on the movie *Planet of the Apes* and the television series *Star Trek*.

Mapping Out Your Treasure Hunt

Your first step toward starting a collection is figuring out what you want to collect. Look around your bedroom. Do you already have two of something, such as sharks' teeth or license plates? Add one more to either pair and you have yourself a small collection. Perhaps you like old things. If you could live in the past, what century would you choose? Maybe you would like to travel back in time by collecting antique tools or toys, cookie cutters, or documents from that historical period.

Browse through an encyclopedia or flip through catalogs of collectibles in a library or bookstore. Search the internet (with your parent's permission) for information and clubs relating to your interest. For example, if you like snow globes, then enter "snow globes" in the search field. You will find a list of websites about these collectibles, where to find different kinds of snow globes, and how to care for them.

There are lots of places to find collectibles. Look in the yellow pages to find specialty stores under these headings: Antiques Dealers, Collectibles, Comic Books, Gift Shops, Hobby Shops, Rock Shops, and Sports Cards. The people working in those shops can give you a lot of information and tell you about local clubs and upcoming events.

Flea markets, swap meets, and conventions are great places to find items to add to and broaden your collection. Arrive early to look at what is available. If you can wait to buy an item, return hours before closing on the final day because many vendors lower prices just before the event ends.

COLLECTIONS   9

TREASURE HUNTS AND PAPER CHASES

Cataloging, Displaying, and Storing a Collection

Properly cataloging your collection is very important for several reasons. It provides essential information for proving the genuineness of your collection. It is a record of financial transactions that you may have to report on an official tax form if you sell your collection for a big profit. It also is a document about your collection that you may need to produce if your collection becomes so valuable that you should carry collectibles insurance.

The records for all the items in your collection make up your *master list*. You might want to keep this information in a three-ring binder or set up an electronic catalog. When you acquire an item for your collection, give it a number. In your master list, record

- The number you gave the item
- A brief description of the item (age, condition, etc.) and a picture (if possible)
- How much you paid for it
- The date and place you acquired it
- The current price guide value
- Any other information that will help explain its significance
- Location of the item (notebook, box, cabinet, etc.)

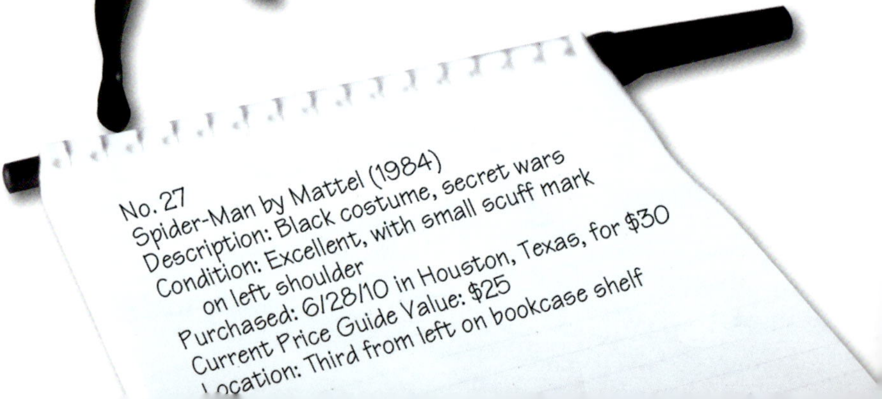

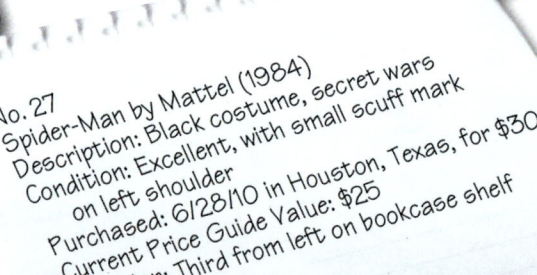

No. 27
Spider-Man by Mattel (1984)
Description: Black costume, secret wars
Condition: Excellent, with small scuff mark on left shoulder
Purchased: 6/28/10 in Houston, Texas, for $30
Current Price Guide Value: $25
Location: Third from left on bookcase shelf

TREASURE HUNTS AND PAPER CHASES

The information you record in your catalog file will depend on the item collected. For example, if the item is a manufactured product, you might record the name of the company and any model or serial numbers. For a limited-edition item, list the number and the size of the edition.

This Wedgewood teacup is the 119th cup produced in a limited edition of 3,000 teacups. Wedgewood is considered one of the finest china companies in the world.

As you hunt for new items to add to your collection, consider carrying a copy of your master list with you. Even if you don't have a large collection yet, you will not have to rely on your memory to know whether an item you already own is graded higher than one you are thinking about buying. Plus you will not accidentally sell one of your items for less than you paid for it.

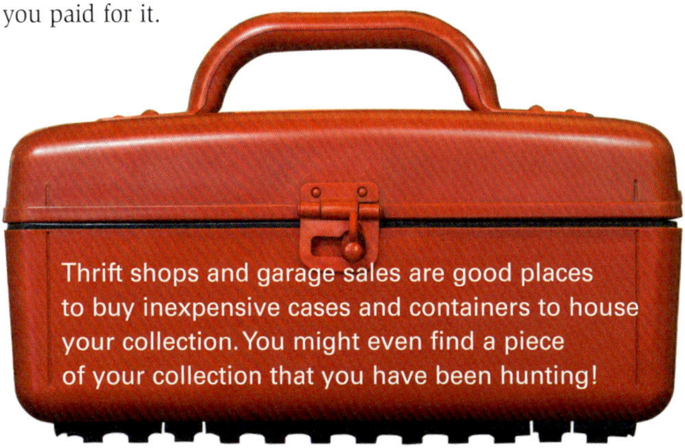

A *limited edition* is the issue of a collectible item—such as a book, art print, medal, or commemorative plate—in a small set quantity.

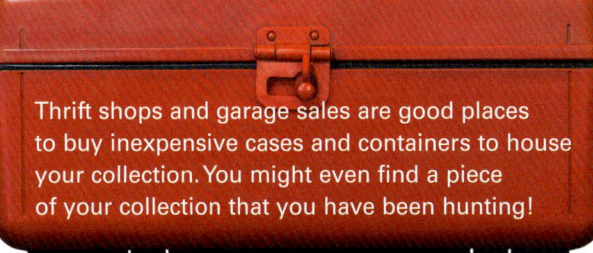

Thrift shops and garage sales are good places to buy inexpensive cases and containers to house your collection. You might even find a piece of your collection that you have been hunting!

COLLECTIONS 11

TREASURE HUNTS AND PAPER CHASES

Display Tips

It is best to keep comic books and sports cards in their protective jackets or in boxes because handling them will decrease their value.

How you display your collection depends on the kind of collection you own. Because of their fragility, certain nature collections such as pressed flowers or leaves should be displayed like framed pictures or mounted on felt boards. Other natural objects such as rocks and fossils can be kept in divided cases or boxes. However, do not keep the boxes under your bed where they are out of sight and out of mind. Part of the fun of having a collection is showing it off and sharing it.

Use your imagination and a little sense of humor (if appropriate) to showcase your collection. Tack a collection of skeleton keys around a doorframe. Display shells in inexpensive bowls or an empty aquarium or showcase a collection of marbles in a recycled divided container meant for assorted chocolates.

> One way to show off and share your collection is by entering contests. Some are sponsored by collectors' clubs, conventions, and even state fairs. Local libraries and historical societies often present personal collections that tie in with their exhibits.

12   COLLECTIONS

Storage Tips

You will want to protect your collection so that it maintains its value and can be enjoyed for many years.

- Store (and display) your collection in a cool, dry place.
- Protect your collectibles from dust, extreme temperatures, and direct sunlight.
- For collectibles such as comic books and sports cards, use a protective polyester film sleeve or a box made with acid-free materials.

> Save the packaging, certificates, and other materials that come with an item, and assign them the same collection number. Collectibles kept in perfect (Mint) condition in their original boxes with all accompanying materials are worth more than the item without its packaging. They are worth even more if the original box has never been opened.

Adhesive labels can damage the surface of your collectible. Instead, write the item's collection number on a piece of paper and keep it in the sleeve or the box.

Store collectibles with moving parts (such as die-cast cars and action figures) or painted items (such as figurines) in individual, divided, and numbered containers. Wrap delicate pieces in soft cloth, bubble wrap, or wadded-up newspaper to prevent scratches and other types of damage. Gently wipe dust from any collectible before storing. If your collectible is stored in a box that is divided into smaller sections, be sure to number each section and put that number in your records.

Depending on its scarcity, the value of a collectible model car could decrease by as much as 50 percent to 75 percent if the paint is scratched or chipped. Take the time to carefully wrap and store your items when they are not on display.

COLLECTIONS   13

Safeguarding Collectibles

- Hand-wash decorated china using only mild soap and warm water.
- Protect paper-based collectibles with acid-free products.
- Ask an expert's advice before cleaning older articles made of fabric or other delicate materials. Store these items in cool, dry locations, and do not seal these collectibles in plastic.
- Avoid abrasives or chemical products such as bleaches or polishes, which could harm your collectible's finish.
- Avoid tampering (this includes refinishing, replating, or restoring) or experimenting with a collectible. Doing so could drastically reduce its value.

Collecting: For Fun or Profit?

Speculation is making a risky purchase based on the hope that you will be able to sell the collectible for a profit.

Everyone has heard stories of rare collectibles that made their owners rich and famous. The hard fact is, most collectibles never bring megabucks when sold. No one knows which collectible will increase in value. So, as you collect, make your purchases with care. Read price guides, specialized catalogs, and collectors' club newsletters. Study auction results, and avoid paying too much for a collectible with the expectation that it will increase in value. It may be years before you can realize a profit.

> The main point of price guides is to provide an extensive list (with photos) of collectible items by category along with suggested purchase prices based on condition. The guides pack a lot more information, too. You will find "state of the market" information about trends and recent sales; articles about the history of the category; warnings about reproductions; lists of upcoming events (auctions, exhibits, seminars, workshops, museum programs); contacts for collectors' clubs; auction announcements; and sale advertisements.

Determining Value: Factors That Matter

A combination of factors determines a collectible's value. Certain factors are more important than others, depending on the type of collectible. For example, if you collect *nostalgia*—sentimental items that remind you of the past—you might be willing to pay more than the item is worth because it has emotional meaning to you. Here are key factors that affect value.

Condition. An item in perfect shape with a like-new appearance will command a top price. It is much more valuable than the same item with flaws.

Authenticity. Do not assume that an item is genuine. Study examples of the real thing, and watch out for reproductions and forgeries. Look for identifying *marks* on the bottom of the item. A signature or date does not guarantee authenticity but should be considered a clue along with information about the design, material, and technique.

Age. An item at least 100 years old is an antique. Age alone does not determine an item's value, but age *and* scarcity, for example, combine for a higher value.

Scarcity. Regardless of age or condition, scarcity does create value because so few items are available. However, certain collectible items produced—and available—in large quantities may be in higher demand because they are more popular than the scarce item.

Provenance. The collectible has documented proof of the history of its ownership. This proof does not guarantee authenticity. Sometimes the value of an item with provenance comes from the celebrity status of a previous owner.

Context. An item has a higher value if it has historical or cultural significance. For example, a posted announcement about an upcoming meeting becomes more valuable if it is related to an important time in history, such as the civil rights movement.

> It usually is best to purchase one really good item rather than buying several slightly flawed pieces.

TREASURE HUNTS AND PAPER CHASES

Invest your time in your collection, not just your money. Read as much as you can about your collectible items. Talk to experienced collectors and dealers. Save your money to purchase one really good item instead of buying several flawed pieces. Build your collection slowly and thoughtfully, adding more valuable pieces as your knowledge increases. Buy what you like, and don't let anyone talk you into selling or trading an item until you are ready.

A *mark,* or hallmark on the bottom of an item such as a china plate or porcelain figurine, provides identifying information: country of origin, manufacturer, age, material, model or pattern, name of the artist. A *touchmark* is the maker's mark impressed on pewter.

Colorful and relatively inexpensive, neckerchiefs from special events and locations are popular with Scout collectors. Other favorite items are neckerchief slides, both the standard metal BSA slides and handcrafted ones.

16   COLLECTIONS

TREASURE HUNTS AND PAPER CHASES

Collecting Scouting Memorabilia

As a Scout, you begin to collect neckerchiefs, pins, and activity patches just by participating. You collect badges that show your rank, council, patrol, and troop number, as well as your completion of merit badge requirements. You might also collect prized patches from Klondike derbies, camporees, and jamborees. Some Scouts also collect handbooks, merit badge pamphlets, and *Boys' Life* magazines. Others prefer Scouting gear such as compasses, canteens, and flashlights.

Scouting-related products from the past include playing cards, board games, bicycle bells, harmonicas, and even a couple of Scouting comic books—*Goofy Scoutmaster* and *Flintstones' Boy Scout Jamboree*. Other Scouting collectibles include Scout banks, paperweights, and coins. Artist Norman Rockwell featured the spirit of Scouting in many of his paintings, which have been reproduced on collectors' plates, mugs, and calendars.

The BSA's 75th and 100th anniversaries in 1985 and 2010 produced additional series of collectibles. If you collect Scouting memorabilia, you may have picked up some new items from the BSA's centennial celebration.

COLLECTIONS

Collecting Odds and Ends

People often assume that collectors are interested only in antiques of great value, such as early American furniture, Chinese porcelain from the Ming dynasty, or paintings by French Impressionists. But many fascinating collections contain the art and objects of everyday life. These items were printed or produced for practical purposes and were not meant to be saved.

Ephemera generally refers to "here today, gone tomorrow" paper collectibles. These include transportation timetables, airplane tickets, sporting event tickets, theatre programs, posters, advertisements and brochures, catalogs, menus, decorated shopping bags, business cards and letterhead, graduation announcements, record album covers, sheet music, valentines and other greeting cards, magazines, and even candy wrappers.

> *Ephemera* are paper collectibles that were originally meant to be thrown away.

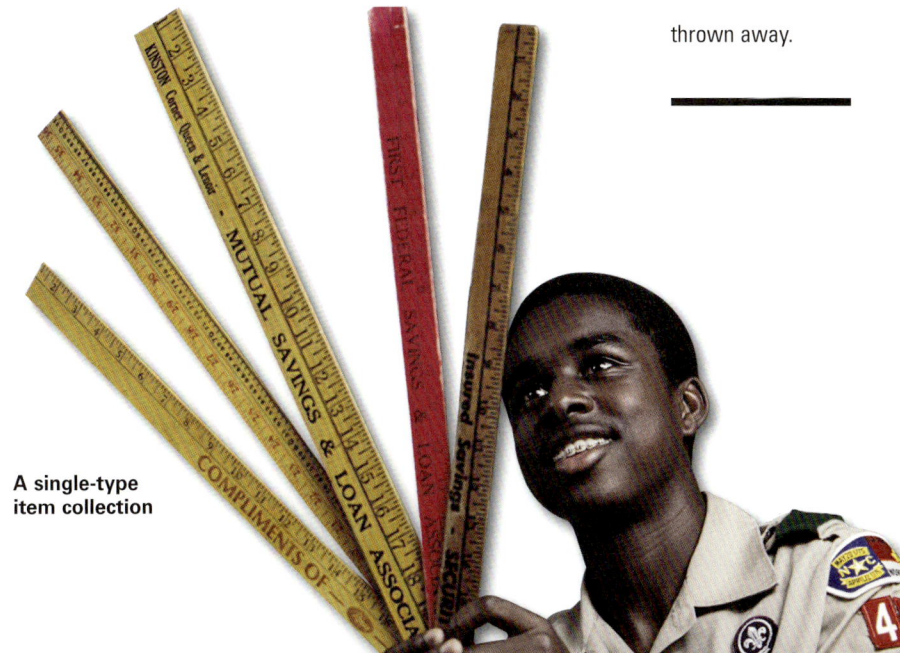

A single-type item collection

COLLECTING ODDS AND ENDS

Dealers and collectors have expanded the field of ephemera to include three-dimensional objects with the same short-lived purpose. Items include pens with company logos, political campaign pin-back buttons, matchbooks, hotel soap, gift or phone cards, and silicone wristbands.

Collectors tend to concentrate on a single type of item (for example, wall calendars) or on all types of items from a specific company, such as Coca-Cola or John Deere.

Rubber wristbands have become popular among collectors.

Advertising Premiums

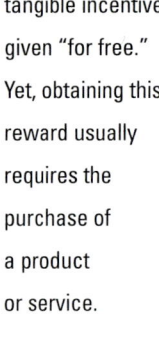

A *premium* is a tangible incentive given "for free." Yet, obtaining this reward usually requires the purchase of a product or service.

Businesses are always trying to find ways to attract customers. One way they advertise is to sponsor a show or event. In the 1920s and 1930s, companies paid to sponsor radio programs aimed at children. They offered free prizes if the kids would send in a box top, label, or other proof of purchase from one of the company's products. In return, the children received a poem, sports ticket, or kid-friendly recipe.

Kids' adventure serials became very popular radio programs. In the 1940s, Ovaltine, a company that produced a chocolate malt–flavored powder for milk, sponsored "Captain Midnight." The company offered special premiums, including a club membership in Captain Midnight's Secret Squadron as well as metal secret-decoder badges.

In 1946, Ovaltine offered this Captain Midnight secret decoder called the "Mirro-Flash Code-O-Graph." Today, this "free" radio premium is valued between $30 and $75, depending on its condition.

COLLECTIONS

Cereal Box Premiums

In the 1950s, cereal companies introduced sugar-coated cereals and targeted them at children. The art on the boxes tied in with licensed TV and cartoon characters such as Batman and the Flintstones. Premiums included on-the-box cutouts for airplanes, masks, and games. Cereal makers discovered that sales of their products related to the popularity of the characters on the boxes.

You can find radio and cereal box premiums at toy and antiques shows, flea markets, and garage sales. Subscribe to hobby newsletters and mail auctions. Talk to dealers and other collectors. Ask what they have for sale, or tell them what you are interested in buying.

Cereal box premiums are popular with young people who commonly eat the cereal as well as with adults.

COLLECTIONS 21

COLLECTING ODDS AND ENDS

Commemorative Ephemera

Some people like to collect *commemorative* items manufactured or printed to honor the memory of a famous person or special event. These souvenirs may include mass-produced items (for example, refrigerator magnets) and high-quality collectibles such as china plates and engraved silver cups. If you build a focused collection of commemorative ephemera, you will learn about the cultural and historical significance of the items as well as discover intriguing information that may inspire you to create "spin-off" collections.

This collection of commemorative ephemera for the 1939 Royal Train Tour of Canada was expanded to include the British king and queen's visit to the United States.

22   COLLECTIONS

COLLECTING ODDS AND ENDS

Collecting Ephemera: Emotional or Financial Investment?

Ephemera collectibles often carry emotional weight. The items may be souvenirs that have great personal meaning, such as toys from loved ones, travel stickers from a family trip across America, or quilts made by your grandmother. You may have a difficult time deciding to sell these items or even putting a value on these "priceless" items. However, people interested in advertising and *Americana* collectibles will have a strong opinion about their value from reading price guides and studying auction results, and from their own experience of buying and selling similar objects.

Americana is a field of collecting that includes objects from or about the United States.

A big factor that affects the value of ephemera is *crossover* appeal. For example, a postcard collector, or *deltiologist,* may be surprised to be involved in a bidding war over a stamped postcard featuring a photo of a painting of a Campbell's soup can. The other bidders include a stamp collector, a Campbell's soup brand collector, and an autograph collector (the postcard writer was the painter). That inexpensive postcard will sell for quite a profit because so many people have different and competitive reasons for acquiring it.

Gene Autry—"the Singing Cowboy"—wrote and recorded hundreds of songs, including "Here Comes Santa Claus," starred in Western films and TV shows, and headlined his own radio program. This pin-back button appeals not only to collectors of pins but also to collectors of comics, sheet music, entertainment, Christmas, and cowboy items.

COLLECTIONS 23

Comic Books: Collecting Superheroes and Villains

The modern-day American comic book is a product of evolution. It began across the Atlantic Ocean more than 500 years ago with a multipanel *broadside* that made fun of religious subjects. Social unrest inspired political cartoons, with the characters' thoughts and speech captured in word balloons. Certain publishers gathered single-panel unrelated cartoons and reprinted them as collections on broadsides. Later, others published sequential multipanels that told a story in oblong strips. In 1818 in Boston, the comic paper called *The Idiot, or Invisible Rambler* introduced the first recurring character that spoke with word balloons.

A *broadside* is a large poster-size sheet of paper printed on one side.

In 1827, Swiss writer and artist Rodolphe Töpffer created a "picture novel" in a small oblong comic strip format. In 1842, American publisher Wilson and Company reformatted Töpffer's *The Adventures of Mr. Obadiah Oldbuck* as a 40-page, 195-panel *graphic novel* to fit its magazine format. Today some people credit Töpffer as the inventor of the modern comic strip and Wilson and Company as the first comic book publisher in America.

A *graphic novel* is a fictional story for adults published as a book in the form of a comic strip.

COLLECTIONS   25

COMIC BOOKS: COLLECTING SUPERHEROES AND VILLAINS

The first sequential comic strips appeared in an American humor magazine in 1852. As the popularity of comics increased, more illustrated humor magazines sprang up. *Puck* was the first to introduce color-tinted cartoons. Newspaper publishers noted the success of those magazines and added "comic supplements" to their Sunday editions to increase their sales.

On May 5, 1895, a New York newspaper reprinted *The Yellow Kid* in color. The cartoon, created by Richard F. Outcault, was originally published in a magazine in black and white. The "Kid" was a goofy-looking, bald-headed boy wearing what looked like a nightgown. Readers loved the colored cartoon *and* the Kid. The cartoonist secured a copyright for his character and licensed all kinds of Yellow Kid items—from toys to appliances to tobacco products. A 196-page comic book called *The Yellow Kid in McFadden's Flats* appeared in 1897.

Richard Outcault's cartoon, *The Yellow Kid*, is considered the forerunner of the modern-day comic book industry, which includes the licensing and merchandising of comic characters.

Publishers in the early 1900s produced comic or "funny" books in all shapes and sizes, with soft- or hardcovers—some even with dust jackets. Most reprinted comic strips from the "funny papers" sections of newspapers.

"Big Little Books" debuted in 1932 with the promise of providing big reading entertainment in a little book. The first title, *The Adventures of Dick Tracy,* sold for 10 cents. These hardcover books were approximately 4 inches square and ran several hundred pages long. The earliest Big Little Books featured reprints of art from newspaper comic strips, with stories adapted to the art.

COLLECTIONS

Because of the commercial success of Outcault's "Yellow Kid" and later his "Buster Brown" comic character as a merchandising mascot for the Buster Brown Shoe Company, many businesses gave away comic strips created to promote their products. In 1933, some employees of the Eastern Color Printing Company (which printed the comic sections for different newspapers) obtained the rights to publish certain comics as a collection in a 32-page color comic magazine. Led by Harry Wildenberg and Maxwell Gaines, the group printed 10,000 copies of *Funnies on Parade* as a premium, or giveaway, for Proctor & Gamble Co. Unlike earlier comic "books," the format of *Funnies on Parade* was actually a quarter-folded newspaper sheet, which made it the size of a magazine similar to modern-day comic books.

In 1934, Eastern published 250,000 copies of *Famous Funnies #1* as a 64-page version of the 32-page giveaway comic magazine. The comic was not free—*Famous Funnies #1* cost 10 cents and was the first comic magazine sold successfully on newsstands. It also became the first monthly comic magazine, lasting 21 years with a peak circulation of 400,000.

The 1930s was a decade of new genres, or types: adventure, science fiction, and detective stories. The "Phantom" was the first hero to appear in a costume; the "Clock" was the first to wear a mask. The Golden Age of comics (and superheroes) began in 1938 when Superman made his first appearance on the cover of *Action Comics #1*. By the mid-40s, more than 400 superheroes followed, including Batman, Captain Marvel, Wonder Woman, and Captain America.

The comic book industry grew quickly during the 1950s, when 1 out of every 3 magazine-type publications sold in America was a comic book. Charles M. Schulz created *Peanuts* in 1955, and the early 1960s gave birth to the *Fantastic Four, Incredible Hulk, X-Men,* and *Amazing Spider-Man.* Then came comic strips based on TV shows and movies, such as *Star Trek* (1967) and *Star Wars* (1977).

COLLECTIONS 27

The Superhero Who Almost Wasn't

In the early 1960s, comic-book writer and editor Stan Lee wanted to develop a superhero with whom the average reader could identify. So he talked to his employer, Marvel Comics, about creating Spider-Man.

"For quite a while, I'd been toying with the idea of doing a strip that would violate all the conventions and break all the rules," Lee said. "A strip that would actually feature a teenager as the star, instead of making him an adult hero's sidekick. A strip in which the main character would lose out as often as he'd win."

At first, the decision makers at Marvel Comics rejected Lee's idea for Spider-Man. They said it would fail because people hated spiders and readers would not want a hero who was an unpopular, pimply high-school student. Marvel Comics finally gave in, and the rest is history.

Spider-Man first appeared in 1962 as a character in the *Amazing Fantasy #15* issue. In March 1963, Spider-Man emerged as the central character under the title *Amazing Spider-Man* and has remained Marvel's leading superhero ever since.

When *Amazing Spider-Man* hit the scene in 1962, it had a unique twist: Spider-Man—the superhero—was not an adult, but a teenager.

COMIC BOOKS: COLLECTING SUPERHEROES AND VILLAINS

Comic Book Ages	
Victorian Age	1828 to 1882
Platinum Age	1883 to 1938
Golden Age	1938 to 1945
Atom Age	1945 to 1956
Silver Age	1956 to 1973
Bronze Age	1973 to 1985
Copper Age	1986 to 1992
Modern Age	1992 to present

The history of comics is defined in terms of ages or eras. These ages often overlap. While not "official," these time periods are considered standard. The beginning of the Golden Age—1938, when Superman first appeared—is the only year on which comic book historians all agree.

Collecting Comics

You can tell from learning about the history of comics that you can collect a variety of comics-related items. Whether you decide to narrow your focus to a specific genre (such as horror or sword-and-sorcery), Silver Age books, or comic character toys, you can find out more by browsing through catalogs, price guides, and collectors' magazines. With your parent's permission, log onto the internet and search for comic book websites.

Talk to enthusiastic employees at comic-book stores. Join a local comic-book club. Attend swap meets and *comicons,* or comic conventions. You will meet other collectors, dealers, publishers, comic-book writers and cartoonists, and professional grading companies. As you learn more about the comic-book industry, you will collect more comics-related things *and* make some friends along the way.

COLLECTIONS

Handling and Storing Comic Books

Comic books are flimsy and can easily be damaged. Most dealers and collectors do not want anyone touching their rare comics because even the smallest crease could reduce a comic's grade from Mint to Near Mint or Very Fine condition. (See the following section about comic book grades.) Always ask permission before handling another person's vintage comic book. Most dealers will remove the comic from its protective sleeve for you so that if the book is damaged, you will not be liable.

Fluorescent light, which has high levels of ultraviolet (UV) radiation, can quickly damage comic books. Even though tungsten filament lighting is less harmful than fluorescent, you should avoid exposing your comics to any light for a long period of time.

When handling valuable comics:

- First wash your hands. The oils from your skin can damage the books.
- Carefully remove the book from its protective sleeve.
- To minimize stress on the book's spine, gently lay the comic flat in the palm of your hand.
- If you have permission to look through the book, carefully turn the pages using your thumb and forefinger. Avoid bending the book open too far.
- When you are through, carefully return the book to its protective sleeve. Watch corners and edges to prevent any damage. If this is not your own comic, ask the dealer or owner to do this so that you will not be responsible for any damage.

Comic Books: Collecting Superheroes and Villains

Comic books are printed on paper—many on cheap paper. Acids used in the production and printing of the books cause the paper to crack and yellow over time. To protect comic books, keep them away from light, heat, extreme cold, and humidity. Improper storage can seriously and permanently deteriorate the condition of your collection.

Place each book in its own acid-free, polyester film sleeve made specifically for long-term storage of comic books. Store the sleeves upright in notebooks or acid-free boxes. As you build your collection, you may want to organize your collection with labeled dividers in labeled notebooks or boxes. For example, you may decide to separate your comics according to historical age, publisher, or genre. Keep your collection in a cool (65 to 70 degrees), dry place away from direct sunlight and fumes. To encourage air circulation and help prevent mold and fungus from developing, be sure to leave a small space between storage boxes and the wall.

> Polypropylene and polyethylene products contain chemicals that can damage your collection over time. These types of sleeves should be used only for temporary storage and should be changed every three to five years.

COLLECTIONS 31

Grading Comic Books

Collectors should know how comic books are graded. A book's economic value is determined by its appearance; one in Poor condition will bring only a fraction of the price of the same one in Mint condition. The condition of the covers, inside pages, and spine all relate to a book's value. Discolored paper, missing portions or pages, fading, tears, markings, brittleness, soiling, and other defects will all diminish the value of the comic book.

Age, scarcity, and physical condition contribute to a comic book's value. The industry uses a complex 10-point grading system that is further broken down into a 25-point range—from .5 for Poor to 10.0 for Gem Mint—to determine the value of a comic book. Here are some guidelines to give you an idea about how comic books are graded.

As you learn about grading, try to obtain the same comic book in different conditions so you can make "apples to apples" comparisons.

Mint (9.9). Condition is nearly perfect, with only subtle binding or printing defects. The cover is flat with no surface wear. Inks are bright with high reflectivity (shininess) and little fading. Corners are square and sharp. The cover is centered and firmly secured. The staples are original and centered, with no rust. The paper is supple (flexible) and fresh. The spine is tight and flat.

Fine (6.0). Condition is above average. The book shows minor wear, but no significant creasing or serious defects. Minor wear on the cover is apparent. The inks show significant loss of reflectivity. Pages or inside covers may have blunted corners and a tan color, but are still supple with no signs of brittleness.

COMIC BOOKS: COLLECTING SUPERHEROES AND VILLAINS

Good (2.0). The comic book has all pages and covers, but small pieces are missing inside. The largest missing piece allowed from the front or back cover is a ½-inch triangle or a ¼-inch square. The book is somewhat creased, scuffed, or soiled, but is still readable. It may have up to a 2-inch split on the spine. The paper quality is low, but not brittle. The cover reflectivity is low or absent. The book has a moderate number of defects, but is still basically sound and whole.

Fair (1.0). The comic book is usually soiled and ragged, with many creases, tears, and folds. The spine is seriously split; the staples are gone. Up to one-tenth of the front cover is missing. Soiling may interfere with one's ability to read the story. The paper quality is low. There is a slight brittleness to the edges of the pages, but not in the center. Coupons have been clipped from pages. The comic book is valued at 50 percent to 70 percent of a copy in Good condition.

Poor (0.5). The comic book is degraded; it is worn, dirty, and torn. The book has severe stains, cover abrasions, and mildew. Its pages are brittle. It is missing staples and pieces of pages. The covers are split from top to bottom, but both halves are present. The value depends on the extent of the defects.

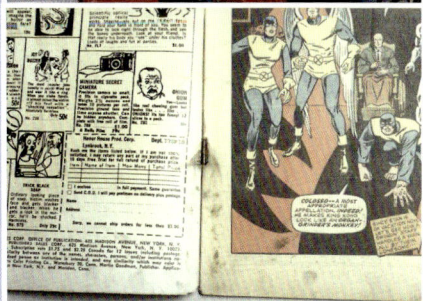

These comics show some moderate defects such as wear, spots, and rusty staples, which affect the comics' value.

Note: The grading descriptions are adapted from *The Official Overstreet Comic Book Grading Guide, 3rd ed.*, with permission from Gemstone Publishing.

COLLECTIONS 33

In the last seven years, third-party companies have offered grading services for valuable comic books. Buyers and sellers recognize the expertise and integrity of these professionals and know that a comic book certified by a professional grader is the real deal. The largest grading company is Certified Guaranty Company (CGC). If you browse through auction catalogs and price guides, you will see comic books listed as "CGC certified" or "CGC graded."

For a fee, you can send your comic book to one of these companies for professional grading. After carefully inspecting your book for wear and tear and signs of *restoration*, the grading specialist will assign a grade, seal your book, and encase it in a *slab* or plastic holder. **Do not unseal the book, or you will invalidate the grading.** Collectors can sell a professionally graded comic book for three to 10 times the amount they would receive for the same nongraded comic.

> A *restored* comic book is one that has had missing or deteriorated pieces replaced or mended so that it appears to be original. Serious collectors do not generally accept this restoration practice because the value of the repaired book is never as high as the original book of the same grade. The seller should always reveal to any potential buyer the restoration of a comic book.

Not every comic book is a good candidate for professional grading because the fees may be higher than the value of the book. The vast majority of comic books are not very valuable. Consider getting your book graded if it meets the following criteria, which may indicate that you have a valuable book that could sell for a big profit.

- Key issue: the first appearance, the story of a character's creation, or any other historical or artistic feature important to collectors
- Debut of a character
- Key first issue
- Deaths of major characters, heroes, or villains
- First work of comic creators who later became popular

Collecting for Laughs or Loot

Before many comic book collectors even thought about putting an organized collection together, they just liked to read comic books. They tended to keep the comics after reading them, and soon they had a stack of books featuring their favorite superhero or favorite adventure or horror series. You may already own a stack of comics. You can call it a collection when you decide to treat your books with respect, organize them, and figure out what others are willing to pay for the issues.

> In 1970, *Action Comics #1* in Mint condition was valued at $300. In 2005, the same comic in Near Mint condition was valued at $485,000. One year later it was valued at $550,000—an increase of $65,000, or 13 percent. Most investors would be happy with that return on investment, and every collector would be thrilled to own the comic book that featured Superman's first appearance and launched the Golden Age of comics.

You can find out the current value of your comics by studying price guides and auction catalogs. While you are looking for information about your own books, you will discover which comics are in high demand and what are the current values for rare comics. Those interesting facts (and high prices!) will inspire you to add to your collection and take care of it.

In 1969, this copy of *The Incredible Hulk* cost 12 cents on the newsstand. Today, in Near Mint condition, the comic is valued at $60.

Cataloging Your Comic Book Collection

Whether you want to collect comics for your own enjoyment or for a chance to make some money, you should keep good records of your collection. At the least, you will know the titles of your comics and how many books you have. If, however, you want to manage your collection and make a profit, you will need to note more specific information.

You can record your information on paper and keep it in a notebook, or create a spreadsheet on the computer. Some companies sell software programs for keeping track of comic book collections. If you note the information for each comic as shown in the following form, you will have a very good record of the description, value, and location of your books.

Here is a sample record from a comic book collection.

Item No.:	47
Title of comic:	Superman: King of the World
Publisher:	DC Comics
Issue No.:	1
Date of issue:	June 1999
Important information:	One-shot, regular edition
Grade or grade abbreviation:	9.2 NM
Additional information about condition:	Paper still fresh; corners square and sharp
Value:	$4.00 as of November 1999
Purchase price:	$3.95
Purchase date:	June 15, 1999
Purchase place:	Nutmeg Comics
Location of Issue:	B4 (box No. 4)

In this example, the comic was issued as a *one-shot*, which means only one issue of that title was published. Regular editions are not mentioned unless other editions of the title—such as collectors' or limited editions—are published.

COMIC BOOKS: COLLECTING SUPERHEROES AND VILLAINS

Item No.:	
Title of comic:	
Publisher:	
Issue No.:	
Date of issue:	
Important information:	
Grade or grade abbreviation:	
Additional information about condition:	
Value:	
Purchase price:	
Purchase date:	
Purchase place:	
Location of Issue:	

Use a chart like this to help catalog your collections. You can modify it any way you like.

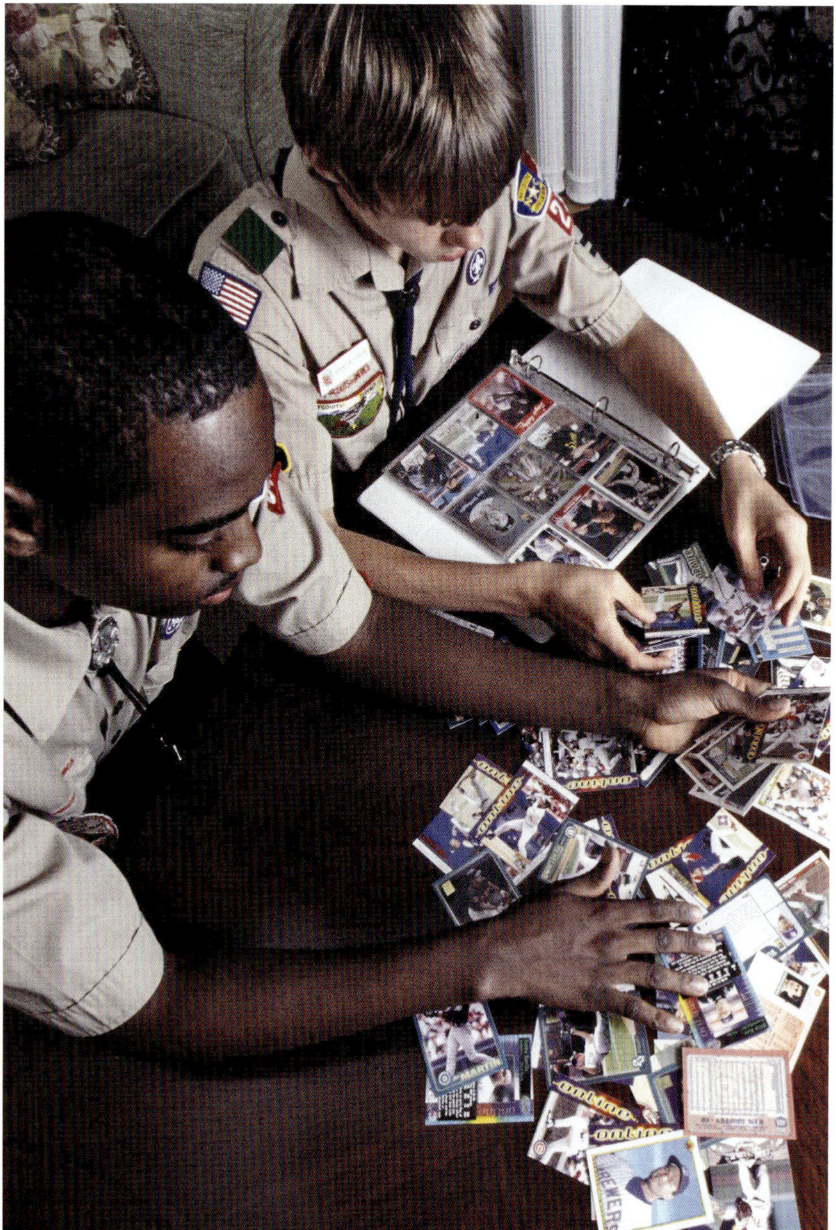

Sports Cards: Collecting Athletes

In 1875, tobacco manufacturer Allen & Ginter of Richmond, Virginia, decided to boost tobacco sales by printing images of athletes, heroes, and other Americans on slender trading cards. The company put individual cards in its packs of cigarettes. The gimmick turned into a wildly successful marketing scheme and launched what is perhaps the first mass marketing of trading cards in the nation.

By 1887, when baseball cards became hot items, several other tobacco companies were packaging similar cards with their own products. Those companies produced some of today's oldest, rarest, and most sought-after sports cards. Ginter is known for the World's Champions series, which featured boxers, baseball players, sharpshooters, pool players, wrestlers, and Wild West heroes Annie Oakley and Buffalo Bill Cody. New York's Goodwin & Co. launched an equally successful Champions series featuring baseball players, bicyclists, weightlifters, marksmen, and college football stars.

What began as an idea to help sell tobacco more than a century ago has grown into a multibillion-dollar industry that includes most major American sports. Today, baseball cards are still the most popular among collectors, followed by cards devoted to football, basketball, and hockey. Every year, hundreds of thousands of sports cards change hands in a huge nationwide network of card dealers, vendors, clubs, and individuals.

Sports Cards: Collecting Athletes

Not all cards are valuable, but they are still fun to collect.

Key cards are the most expensive, desirable, or important cards.

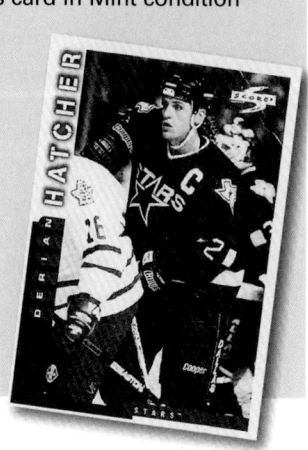

The Top Sports Cards

Here are a few of the most valuable sports cards.

Baseball
1915 Sporting News #151, Babe Ruth, Boston Red Sox
Importance: Babe Ruth's rookie card

1932 U.S. Caramel #26, Lou Gehrig, New York Yankees
Importance: The first key Lou Gehrig card

Basketball
1969 Topps #25, Lew Alcindor (Kareem Abdul-Jabbar), Milwaukee Bucks
Importance: The star's only recognized rookie card

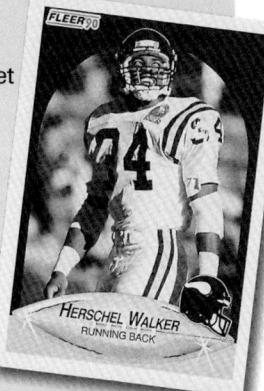

Boxing
1948 Leaf #1, Jack Dempsey
Importance: First card in the set featuring the boxer

Football
1933 Goudey Sport Kings, Red Grange, Chicago Bears
Importance: Good color features; appealing image

Golf
1998 Champions of Golf Master Collection, Tiger Woods
Importance: Tough to find this card in Mint condition

Hockey
1951 Parkhurst #4, Maurice Richard, Montreal Canadiens
Importance: Richard's only recognized rookie card

1979 O-Pee-Chee #18, Wayne Gretzky, Edmonton Oilers
Importance: Gretzky's key rookie card

COLLECTIONS

Grading Sports Cards

A sports card is graded based on its condition—a factor often more important in setting its value than the player on the card. In Poor condition, a card typically will be valued at least 20 percent lower than the same card in Good condition. No slack is given to older cards—a card 40 years old is judged by the same standards as one from the last sports season.

Besides the creases, folds, tears, and angled or off-centered photos that drastically reduce a card's value, minor flaws can hurt value, too. Depending on their seriousness, the following flaws may lower a card's value by one to four grades: bubbles (lumps in the surface), gum and wax stains, diamond cutting (slanted borders), notching, paper wrinkles, scratched-off cartoons or puzzles on the back, rubber-band marks, surface impressions, and warping.

Most card injuries begin at the corners. Experts who rate cards give five different grades to the conditions of a card's corners. The more rounded and worn the corners, the lower the grade.

The corners of a single card could be rated in different categories. These are the major categories of corner wear.*

Sharp. The corner is sharp, but shows slight wear. On a dark-bordered card, this wearing shows as a dot of white.

Fuzzy. The corner comes to a right angle, but that angle shows a little fraying. A slightly dinged (nicked) corner is considered the same as a fuzzy corner.

Slightly Rounded. Fraying at a corner has led to a rounding of the edge. The corner may show layering where the card's paper stock is split.

Rounded. The corners are rounded and there is some layering.

Badly Rounded. The corners are completely rounded and the layering is severe.

*From *Beckett Almanac of Baseball Cards and Collectibles No. 7,* ©2002 Beckett Publications. Reprinted with permission.

Different professional grading companies have their own numeric codes for evaluating the conditions of sports cards, but all are based on general guidelines from Mint to Poor.

Mint. A card with no flaws or wear; it has four perfect corners. The card has excellent centering of the picture. It has retained its original gloss (shine), smooth edges, and original color borders. There are no printing defects (spots or lines), or color or focus imperfections.

Near Mint. The card has one minor flaw. Flaws that would lower the card's rating: one fuzzy corner or two to four corners with slight wear, nearly perfect centering, minor print spots.

Excellent. The card has four fuzzy but not rounded corners. The centering is no worse than 80/20 (the card's picture is off-center, with up to 80 percent of the border shifted to one side of the picture and 20 percent or more on the opposite side). There is minimal loss of the original gloss, with rough edges, slightly discolored borders, and minor print spots.

Very Good. The card has been handled but not abused. Its corners are slightly rounded and slightly layered. There is slight notching on the edges. The card shows significant gloss loss from the surface, but no scuffing. The card shows moderate discoloration on the borders. The card may have a few light creases.

Good, Fair, Poor. The card is worn or has been mishandled or abused. The corners are badly rounded and layered. There is scuffing, and most or all of the original gloss is gone. There are seriously discolored borders, moderate or heavy creases, and one or more serious flaws.

Note: This information comes from *Beckett Almanac of Baseball Cards and Collectibles No. 7,* ©2002 Beckett Publications, and is reprinted with permission.

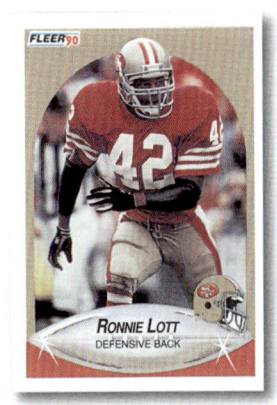

Sports Cards: Collecting Athletes

Mint condition 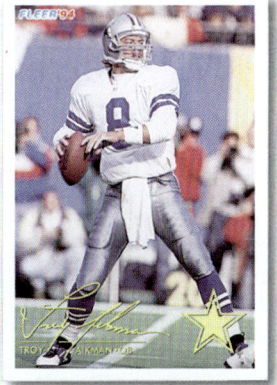 **Very Good condition** 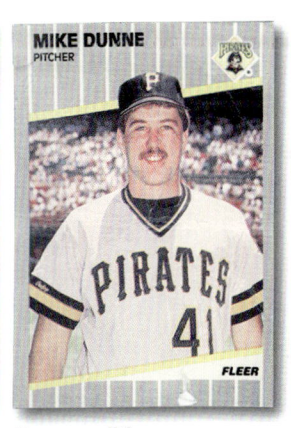 **Poor condition**

Many hobbyists have widened their collections to include items such as cereal boxes, autographed programs, and gameday tickets. However, autographs can sometimes *reduce* a sports card's value. If you want to collect an autograph, ask the player to sign a spare card or another item.

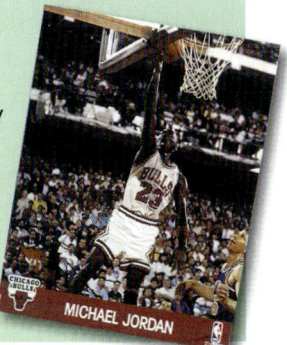

Value is also based on supply and demand. For those who collect only Mint-condition cards, the supply of older cards may be quite small. Each year some cards are thrown away, lost, or otherwise destroyed, reducing the supply. Until recently, only serious collectors realized the need to preserve cards to hold their value.

Demand depends on the interest of individual collectors, fads, trends, and other factors. It is governed mostly by the age of the card, the number of cards printed, the player shown on the card, the attractiveness and popularity of the set, and the card's condition In other words: The older the card, the fewer the number, the more famous the player, the more attractive the set, the better the condition—the higher the value.

The Real Deal

Many collectors have felt the sting of unknowingly buying trimmed, recolored, or counterfeit cards. Spotting fakes can be hard, so take these precautions and consult pricing guides for other tips.

- Carefully inspect a card's dot pattern. Cards are printed on high-speed presses that use dots of ink to make the picture. Use a 16x (16-power) magnifier to inspect the printing, especially the black areas and any dark text. If possible, compare the card to a known genuine sample. Fake cards usually are rescreened, indicating they have been copied (making a card's solid-ink areas look blurry under a magnifier). Also beware of blurry or faded photos.

- Recolored cards typically have damaged or chipped edges or surface dings. Look at the edges, under magnification, for ink bleeding. This happens when ink used to recolor a chipped edge or spot "bleeds" from the surface of the card's paper onto the edge itself. It is hard for someone to recolor a card without leaving the telltale evidence.

- Retouched cards might have poorly shaved edges. The edge often appears too smooth, too rough, or too closely trimmed. Detecting a shaved edge can be tricky.

- A card's edge is sometimes its most telling feature. Tampered cards may have *beveled* edges. Under magnification and from the side, a beveled edge will show an outward slant that is not used in the original trimming of a card.

Collecting Sports Cards: Trading and Buying

Some people collect complete sets of cards for an athlete's entire career. Others focus on a particular team or collect the first, or rookie, cards of players who have gone on to become standouts in their sport. You can buy cards in different combinations—as individual cards or as a pack, box, or set. Let your own interests (and your budget) guide your decisions as you put your collection together.

Serious collectors get cards from various sources: other collectors or dealers, sale or auction ads in hobby publications, local hobby stores, sports collectibles shows or conventions, or the internet marketplace. Professionals suggest that collectors try all five sources, but be a smart shopper. Just as department stores unload summer clothes in the fall, card dealers do the same. They often clear out a current year's cards at reduced prices after the end of a particular sport's season.

At card shows or conventions, hundreds of vendors display thousands of cards from various sports. You can learn a lot about sports-card collecting at these events, such as how to figure out the value of cards, how to organize your collection, and how to sell for a profit

Monthly collectibles magazines found on most newsstands offer state-by-state listings of related conventions and shows.

Learn more about collecting sports cards or about specific cards by browsing the internet (with your parent's permission). Log onto a good search engine and key in terms of interest, such as "football cards" or "Miami Dolphins"—using words that describe the cards or information you seek. There are countless websites devoted to the history of collecting, to a particular era, or to specific players.

Storing and Organizing Your Cards

Sleeves come in different sizes. Be sure your cards fit snugly in their sleeves so that they stay put when handled.

Now that you know how the condition of a card affects its value, you understand the importance of caring for your sports cards. Use protective sleeves to hold cards. Buy only sleeves made of polyester film and advertised as "acid free," because acid and other chemicals can harm paper items over time. You can find these protective products in hobby and collectibles shops and on the internet (with your parent's permission, of course).

Use common sense when storing your collection. Keep the cards in a cool, dry place away from direct sunlight, extreme temperatures, and fumes. Do not store your collection in an attic, garage, or damp basement.

These storage sleeves make viewing easy.

Cataloging Your Collection

Whether you store your cards in albums or boxes, you will have a hard time finding a specific one if you do not keep records. If you take the time to list your cards—on paper or on the computer—you will avoid buying or trading identical cards in the same condition. Plus, if you do decide to sell a card, you will know what you paid for it and its current market value.

Sports Cards: Collecting Athletes

Here is a sample record from a sports card collection.

Item No.:	638	Card No:	55
Sport:	Baseball	Date of issue:	February 2, 1999
Team:	New York Yankees	Condition:	Good
Player:	Babe Ruth	Value:	$2.50 as of August 1999
Position:	First base	Purchase price:	$1.00
Series:	Yankees Hall of Fame	Purchase date:	March 4, 1999
Information:	Theme: Power Hitters	Purchase place:	Deke's Sports Cards
Brand:	Fleer	Location of card:	A4 (album No. 4)

Item No.:		Card No:	
Sport:		Date of issue:	
Team:		Condition:	
Player:		Value:	
Position:		Purchase price:	
Series:		Purchase date:	
Information:		Purchase place:	
Brand:		Location of card:	

Organize your records to track the information you want to know. You can use a form like this one or buy computer software for cataloging sports cards.

COLLECTIONS 47

The cards you collect reflect your personality. They show what athletes you admire, what sports you enjoy, what playing positions interest you, and they might even reveal what goals you have for your future.

For Love or Money: Keeping or Selling Your Cards

Sports card collecting is a personal pastime, but the sports card industry is big business. Players earn money for having their pictures featured. The sports leagues in which they play get royalties for the use of the league names and logos. Card companies make money producing and selling cards. Sometimes, collectors make a lot of money, too.

In 1909, Pittsburgh Pirates shortstop Honus Wagner created a ruckus about his image being used on a sports card. One story claims he demanded his image be removed from tobacco-sponsored cards because he believed the cards encouraged children to use tobacco. Another story says Wagner was upset because he thought he should be paid part of the profits that his cards earned. To avoid Wagner's legal action, the card company destroyed nearly all of his cards. Today, Wagner cards are among the rarest. In 2000, a California collector paid $1.1 million for a Near Mint 1909 Wagner card.

Sports cards like this 1953 Topps #317 Hank Aaron often are paired with other collectibles in a handsome display, making the hobby more interesting and fun to show off.

COLLECTIONS

SPORTS CARDS: COLLECTING ATHLETES

Even though you might like to make a profit by selling your sports cards, remember to enjoy this hobby. Buy what you like—in the best condition you can afford. Take care of your cards and keep good records, but always have fun.

> Here are some other valuable baseball cards. The values are estimated market prices for cards in Mint or Near Mint conditions.
>
> 1952 Topps #311 Mickey Mantle—$66,887
> 1933 Goudey #106 Nap Lajoie—$55,152
> 1914 E145-1 Cracker Jack #103 Joe Jackson—$22,800
> 1949 Leaf #8 Satchel Paige—$12,000
> 1951 Bowman #305 Willie Mays—$9,860
> 1954 Bowman #66A Ted Williams—$7,853
> 1938 Goudey Heads Up #274 Joe DiMaggio—$7,663

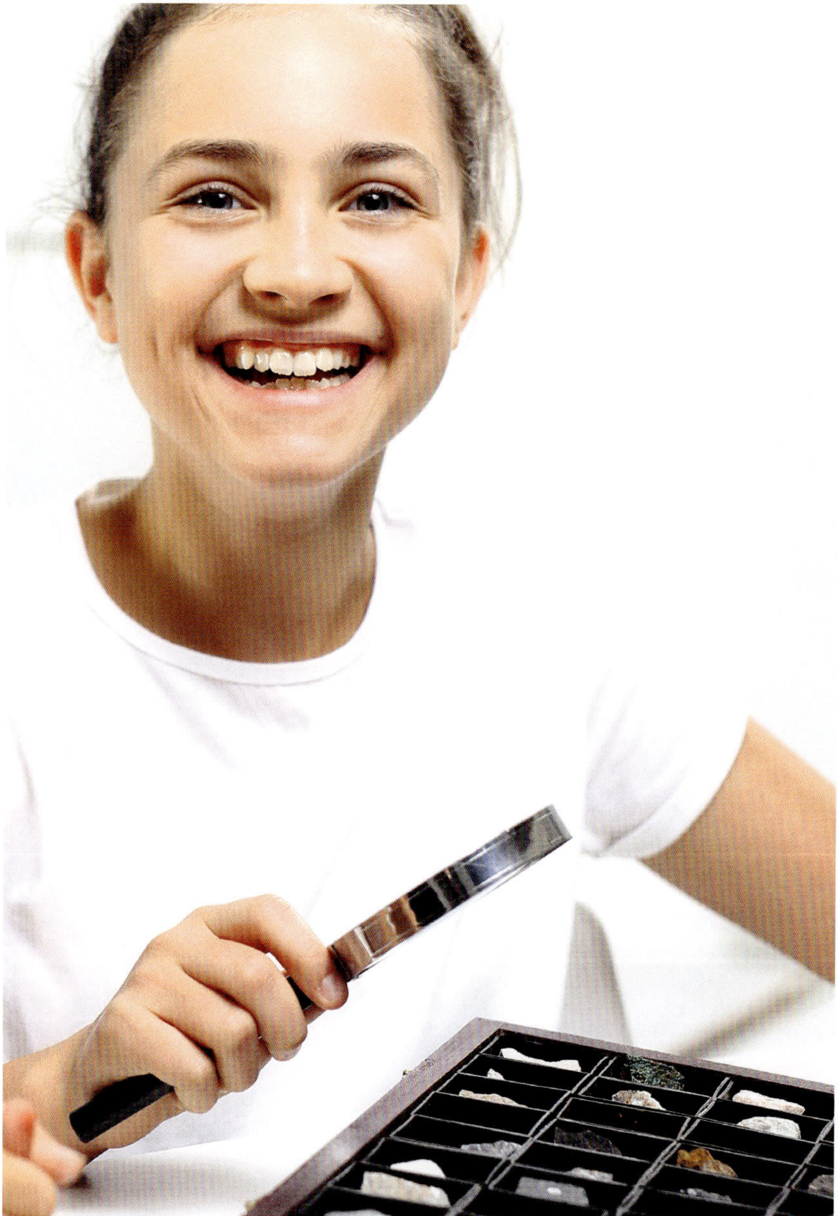

Rocks: Collecting Chunks of the Past

Rock hounds have long been fascinated with rocks because they are evidence of the physical forces that have altered the face of our planet. Wind and water ravage Earth's surface, wearing down mountains and reducing pebbles to sand. Meanwhile—below Earth's surface—the temperature rises so dramatically that rock melts. These processes, which scientists believe may have been happening for billions of years, are never-ending. People collect rocks that reveal Earth's natural history even as the rocks of the future are being formed.

As a beginning rock collector, you can decide to base your collection on a number of factors, like color, shape, texture, or anything that strikes your interest. As your interest in the rocks' origin and identification grows, you can begin to learn more about different rock classifications.

A *rock hound* is an amateur collector of rocks and minerals.

Finding and Collecting Rocks

You do not have to go much farther than your driveway to start a common rock collection. Better sites, though, are where you find cuts in rocks made by humans: quarries, mines, and road building and construction sites. The best sites are where rock has been recently exposed, such as valley floors and the bottoms of mountain streams. If you plan to identify the rocks from their texture and mineralogical features, try to collect samples about the size of your fist.

Rocks: Collecting Chunks of the Past

If you will be rock hunting on private property, get the landowner's or land manager's permission. Do not disturb wildlife, livestock, fences, or other property. Remember, it is illegal to collect rocks in state parks, national parks, or national monuments. You may collect rocks immediately outside these areas only if you have permission.

Many rock hounds try to collect all the related rocks from the area in which they live. Others collect *micromounts*—very small mineral specimens that are usually the size of a fingernail.

Consider joining a rock and mineral club, or subscribe to a rock and mineral magazine, to learn what others collect and how to expand your own collection. Besides having information about local rock and gem shows, many rock clubs and societies offer workshops on topics such as cleaning and organizing specimens and understanding rock formations and crystal structures.

Rock and gem shows are excellent places to buy or trade specimens. Many natural museums have rock and mineral displays, and also sell starter kits in their gift shops.

Tip: When you are out rock hunting, collect extra specimens that you can trade with other rock hounds to fill gaps in your collection.

ROCKS: COLLECTING CHUNKS OF THE PAST

Rockhounding Tools

Every beginning rock collector should try to get two pieces of specialized equipment: a geologist's hammer and a hand lens. Use the hammer to break off rock specimens and trim them to display size. Hammer with the blunt end and chisel with the pick end. You can purchase a geologist's hammer in scientific supply houses or specialty stores.

Once you have a rock in hand, you will need a lens or pocket magnifier to identify the specimen's mineral grains. Six-power to 10-power magnification is best. Advanced collectors use an optically corrected lens. Beginners can start with hand lenses, which may be purchased in jewelry stores, optical shops, or scientific supply houses.

While rock collecting, you may need some or all of this equipment: field guide to rocks and minerals, geologist's hammer, chisel, small hand trowel, magnifying glass, compass, map, pocketknife, hard hat, safety glasses, gloves, knapsack, camera, newspaper to wrap rocks, adhesive tape to make a temporary label, felt-tip marker.

> **!** If you plan to chisel or hammer rock to get individual specimens, wear safety glasses. Striking rocks with a hammer may knock off sharp chips that could seriously injure your unprotected eyes.

COLLECTIONS 53

Safety Tips

- Never enter an abandoned mine. Walls frequently collapse.
- Wear a hard hat when hunting below a rock face.
- If chiseling rock for specimens, wear protective eyewear.
- Wear gloves and sturdy boots or shoes.
- Always carry a compass and a good map, and know how to use them.
- Whether you are collecting alone or with a friend, always make sure someone knows where you are going.
- Never throw rocks off a ledge—someone might be right below.

If you keep your specimens on trays, place a small card with identifying information beneath each rock for quick reference.

Cataloging and Displaying Rocks

Record specimens in a field notebook as you collect the rocks. Although fully identifying a sample can wait until later, you should immediately date and label your rock and note the location where you found it. Use a piece of adhesive tape and a marker to make a temporary label. Many collections become mixed up because collectors fail to do this.

Just as in any field of collecting, a labeling system is critical. Many rock collectors dab white water-soluble paint or lacquer on a corner of each specimen, then write a reference number on the paint with a black felt tip pen. For tiny samples, mark the numbers on the container in which you keep the specimens.

ROCKS: COLLECTING CHUNKS OF THE PAST

Most rocks rarely require special treatment. Soak your specimens in cold water and (if they are not too delicate) clean them with an old toothbrush. Allow them to air dry. You can simply store a rock collection in shoe boxes or corrugated cardboard boxes or display it on shelves.

Egg cartons make excellent containers for smaller rock specimens. If you want something fancier, use cases that have individual compartments and glass lids.

Rocks: Collecting Chunks of the Past

In your own notebook, record the specimen's number and name, date you collected the rock, description of the collection site, and other relevant data. If you bought the rock, note the seller's name, purchase price, and purchase date.

For more information on identifying rocks, see the *Geology* merit badge pamphlet.

Evaluating Your Collection

Determining the value of a nonprecious rock or mineral collection can be difficult because there are no price guides available as there are for other kinds of collectibles. Often the price of common rocks such as granite or limestone is quoted per pound. To get a general idea of the value of your rocks, go to rock and mineral shows or to rock shops to find out what people are charging for similar specimens.

Dealers and other collectors might be interested in buying some of your rocks if you have a rare one found only in a remote part of the world. Perhaps you have some unique crystals that are special for their clarity, shape, and color. In any case, you would have to negotiate a price based on your knowledge of comparable rock sales.

56 COLLECTIONS

ROCKS: COLLECTING CHUNKS OF THE PAST

You can find buyer's guides for gemstones. Also, if you have precious or semiprecious gemstones (opals, corundum sapphires) in your collection, you can take them to a gemstone appraiser to find out what the stones are worth (for a fee). The appraiser is trained to grade the gemstones in terms of appearance, quality, rarity, weight, and other factors that make it unique.

Most rocks and minerals you find "in the field" have little cash value, but they are important for what they represent in your collection. As you show your collection to other rock hounds, you will discover that your rocks are worth something: first, when they admire your samples; and second, when they ask to trade specimens or offer you money for a rock they need in their own collection.

$22.95 each
RIDDELL MINI HELMET
$22.95 each
ELWAY
EACH
$10.00
50¢ EACH FOOTBALL
25 FOR $10.00
FOOTBALL
50¢ EACH
$10 FOR 25

Careers: From Hobby to Profession

Some people use their hobby to relax after work. Others work at their hobby. You can take many different career paths that relate to your interest in collecting. For certain occupations—such as dealing in comics-related merchandise—you can jump right into a business if you have a collection to sell, a place to store it, money to travel and buy more inventory, ways to sell merchandise (webpage or auctions on the internet, storefront, booth at a show), and some understanding about financial record-keeping and tax laws.

Many dealers are self-taught. They may have a deep knowledge and obvious enthusiasm about their products from years of passionate collecting and research. They have also built a network of potential clients and contacts from attending club meetings, conventions, and auctions.

You may be more interested in creating comic books than selling them. If you have artistic talent, you can be—with some training—a cartoonist, penciller, colorist, or inker. There are a number of career opportunities in comic book publishing. Grading comic books also can be a rewarding area to pursue.

> Your interest in collecting sports cards may lead you into playing sports, sportscasting or sportswriting, or creating sports card packaging and promotions.

Careers: From Hobby to Profession

One Scout started his collection with a few hand-forged nails from his grandfather's barn. As his collection grew, he built a career supplying hardware for authentic restorations.

Rock collectors with a strong scientific curiosity may pursue careers as mineralogists, petrologists, geologists, or teachers. Rock hounds with a particular interest in gemstones may become gemologists (trained in gemstone identification and grading), appraisers, diamond cutters, lapidaries (artisans who work with precious and semiprecious stones and minerals), bench jewelers (professionals who make, repair, and adjust jewelry), or jewelry designers.

Robert Haag, also known as the Meteorite Man, used to go with his parents on prospecting trips to the Arizona desert. He became a rock hound and studied geology in college. Today, he travels the world collecting meteorites to buy, sell, and trade. In a vault beneath his home in Tucson, he keeps a treasure of meteorites, including pieces of the moon and Mars.

CAREERS: FROM HOBBY TO PROFESSION

A whole industry exists to support the buying, selling, and display and preservation of collectibles. Auction houses, galleries, and museums employ auctioneers, appraisers, curators, and conservators. People hired for these positions often specialize in one area, such as pottery and porcelain or prints and paintings.

You can turn any collecting interest into a related career. For example, your candy dispensers collection may inspire you to become a toy manufacturer, candy-maker, pop culture historian, hobby magazine writer, brand manager, or product placement specialist.

Education and Training

A collector is a narrowly focused expert, and that is sometimes enough to get started. Often, however, more schooling and training are necessary because so much is at stake. Find out from people in your collection network what they had to study, specialized schools they had to attend, skills they had to learn, and professional organizations they joined to prepare for their career.

Talk to your school counselor about some of the positions mentioned above and discuss which colleges or trade schools might offer the courses and training you will need. As you consider your future, start a new collection—your own career choices.

COLLECTIONS

Resources for Collecting

Scouting Literature
Archeology, Basketry, Coin Collecting, Fishing, Fly-Fishing, Geology, Graphic Arts, Indian Lore, Journalism, Leatherwork, Metalwork, Painting, Photography, Pottery, Pulp and Paper, Railroading, Reading, Scouting Heritage, Sculpture, Sports, Stamp Collecting, Textile, Theater, Wood Carving, and *Woodwork* merit badge pamphlets

> With your parent's permission, visit the Boy Scouts of America's official retail website, www.scoutshop.org, for a complete listing of all merit badge pamphlets and other helpful Scouting materials and supplies.

Books
Baker, H.K.G. *Cool Collectibles for Kids: A Kid's and Parent's Guide to the Hobby of Collecting.* Silverleaf Press, 2007.

Beckett, James. *Beckett Almanac of Baseball Cards and Collectibles,* 2006 ed., Vol.11. Beckett Publications, 2006. (Beckett writes price guides for all the major sports cards.)

Berg, Barry. *The Art of Buying and Selling at Flea Markets.* Hobby House Press, 2003.

Collector Books. *Garage Sale Flea Market Annual: Current Values on Today's Collectibles, Tomorrow's Antiques.* Collector Books, 2006.

Farndon, John. *The Practical Encyclopedia of Rocks and Minerals: How to Find, Identify, Collect, and Maintain the World's Best Specimens.* Lorenz Books, 2006.

Gerber, Ernst. *The Photo-Journal Guide to Comic Books* (2 vols.). Diamond Comic Distributors, 1995.

Hake, Ted. *The Official Hake's Price Guide to Character Toys,* 6th ed. House of Collectibles, 2006.

Lemke, Bob, ed. *2007 Standard Catalog of Baseball Cards,* 16th ed. Krause Publications, 2006. (Krause also publishes catalogs covering other sports.)

MacDonald-Taylor, Margaret. *A Dictionary of Marks,* 5th ed. Barrie and Jenkins, 1992.

Newell, Patrick. *Cool Collectibles: Military Collectibles.* Children's Press, 2000.

Nigro, Nicholas J. *The Everything Collectibles Book: How to Buy and Sell Your Favorite Treasures, From Fabulous Flea Market Finds to Incredible Online Deals.* Adams Media, 2002.

Overstreet, Robert M. *The Official Overstreet Comic Book Price Guide*, 37th ed. House of Collectibles, 2007.

Prisant, Carol. *Antiques Roadshow Collectibles: The Complete Guide to Collecting 20th Century Glassware, Costume Jewelry, Memorabilia, Toys, and More From the Most-Watched Show on PBS*. Workman Publishing Company, 2003.

Rickards, Maurice. *Encyclopedia of Ephemera*. Routledge, 2000.

Sorrell, Charles A. *Rocks and Minerals: A Guide to Field Identification*. Golden Guides for St. Martin's Press, 2001.

Stearns, Dan, ed. *Standard Catalog of Die-Cast Vehicles*. Krause Publications, 2005.

Summers, B.J. *Antique and Contemporary Advertising Memorabilia*, 2nd ed. Collector Books, 2004.

Thompson, Maggie, et al. *2007 Comic Book Checklist and Price Guide: 1961 to Present*, 13th ed. Krause Publications, 2006.

Williams, Don, and Louisa Jaggar. *Saving Stuff: How to Care for and Preserve Your Collectibles, Heirlooms, and Other Prized Possessions*. Fireside, 2005.

Organizations and Websites

Association of Collecting Clubs and National Association of Collectors
18222 Flower Hill Way, No. 229
Gaithersburg, MD 20879
Website: http://collectors.org

Ephemera Society of America
P.O. Box 95
Cazenovia, NY 13035-0095
Telephone: 315-655-9139
Website: http://www.ephemerasociety.org

International Scouting Collectors Association
Website: http://scouttrader.org

Lepidopterists' Society
Website: http://www.lepsoc.org

Printed Ephemera Collection at Library of Congress
Website: http://memory.loc.gov/ammem/rbpehtml/pehome.html

Smithsonian Center for Education and Museum Studies
P.O. Box 37012, MRC 508
Washington, DC 20013-7012
Telephone: 202-633-5330
Website: www.smithsonianeducation.org/idealabs/collecting/

Society of Illustrators
128 E. 63rd St.
New York, NY 10065
Telephone: 212-838-2560
Website: http://societyillustrators.org

United States Club List
Website: http://www.rockhounds.com/rockshop/clublist.html

Magazines and Publishers

Beckett Media
Website: http://www.beckett.com

Comics Buyer's Guide
Website: http://www.cbgxtra.com

DC Comics
Website: http://www.dccomics.com

Gemstone Publishing
Website: http://www.gemstonepub.com

Resources for Collecting

Marvel Comics
Website: http://www.marvel.com

Panini Sports Trading Cards
Website: http://www.donruss.com

Rocks & Minerals
Website: http://www.rocksandminerals.org

Topps
Website: http://www.topps.com

Trading Card Central
Website: http://www.tradingcardcentral.com

Tuff Stuff (a multisports collectibles magazine)
Website: http://www.tuffstuff.com

Upper Deck
Website: http://www.upperdeck.com

Acknowledgments

The Boy Scouts of America thanks Dr. and Mrs. Charles Deur, Arlington, Texas, for th[...] shoot for th[...] and for sh[...] about colle[...]

The B[...] to the mer[...] National [...] for the im[...] this pampl[...]

Photo a[...]

C.S. Dixo[...] page 9[...]
Footballca[...]
HeritageC[...] 27–28[...]

Shutterstock.com—cover (*geode*, ©michal812; *van*, ©jantarus); pages 4 (©charles taylor), 6 (©AboutLife), 7 (*jar*, ©Jim Hughes; *marbles*, ©arosoft), 8 (*butterfly*, ©Butterfly Hunter), 11 (*red box*, ©Mathisa), 14 (*red car*, ©Burachet; *blue* and *pink cars*, ©Andreas Gradin), 15 (©Viktor1), 18 (*stamps*, ©LSkywalker; *tickets*, ©AKaiser; *marbles*, ©TOMO; *corks*, ©Discovod; *shells*, ©Vibe Images), 23 (*license plates*, ©Cameron Cross), 30 (©goodluz), 44 (*magnifying glass*, ©stockCe), 50 (©Robert Przybysz), 51 (©Ivan Smuk), 52 (*pebbles*, ©Diana Taliun; *rock collection*, ©Zigzag Mountain Art), 56 (*crystals*, ©Archiwiz), 57 (*semiprecious stones*, ©Natali Glado), 59 (©Rawpixel), and 60 (*crater*, ©wassiliyarchitect)

Syracuse University Library, Syracuse, New York, courtesy—page 26

[...]er (*baseball*[...]0 (*all*)[...]ne)[...]e,[...]41[...] of or are[...]merica.

[...]igure);[...]re,[...], 32–33

[...]dan),[...]nifying[...])